GEMINI

MAY 21–JUNE 20

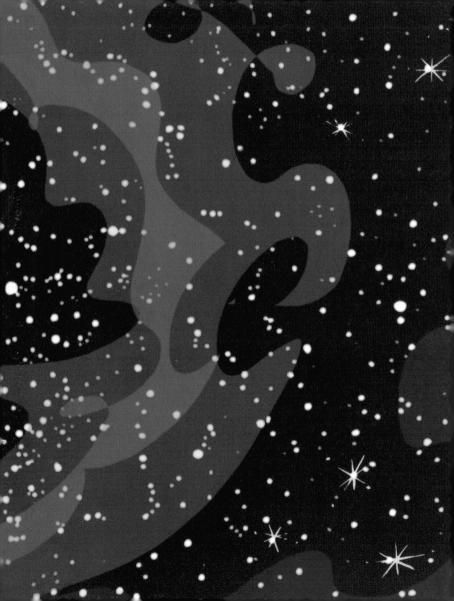

· JUNIOR ASTROLOGER ·

GEMINI

MAY 21–JUNE 20

ALEXIS QUINLAN

ILLUSTRATIONS BY IRENE ROFHEART PIGOTT

CADER BOOKS • NEW YORK

Andrews and McMeel
Kansas City

Thank you for buying this Cader Book—we hope you enjoy it.
And thanks as well to the store that sold you this, and the hardworking
sales rep who sold it to them. It takes a lot of people to make a book.
Here are some of the people who were instrumental:

Editorial: Jackie Kramer, Jake Morrissey, Dorothy O'Brien,
Regan Brown, Nora Donaghy
Design: Charles Kreloff
Copy Editing/Proofing: Bill Bryan
Production: Carol Coe, Traci Bertz, Cathy Kirkland
Legal: Renee Schwartz, Esq.

Printed in China.

If you would like to share any thoughts about this book, or are interested in other
books by us, please write to: Cader Books, 38 E. 29 Street, New York, NY 10016.

Or visit our web site: http://www.caderbooks.com

Library of Congress Catalog Card Number: 96-79247

June 1997

First Edition

10 9 8 7 6 5 4 3 2 1

Attention Schools and Businesses: Andrews and McMeel books are available for
educational, business, or sales promotional use. For information, please write to:
Special Sales Department, Andrews and McMeel, 4520 Main Street,
Kansas City, Missouri 64111

TO DEREK MARLOWE
FRIEND
SHORTWAVE RADIO
INSPIRING SCRIBBLER

CONTENTS

**Psst!
Looking for
predictions? Sorry.
The best astrologers
know that the stars don't
make things happen—
people do! (But if you
must have your
fortune told, turn
to page 64.)**

WELCOME TO ZODIAC ZONE

Imagine our world without skyscrapers, highways, or malls to block the horizon. Imagine our planet without flashing signs or neon lights to compete with the brightness above. It's just you and the great sky: the fiery sun blazing above every day, the moody moon changing its shape all month long, and the glittery planets and stars bedazzling the sky every night.

That's how it was 5,000 years ago, in the ancient city of Babylon. There, in the cradle of civilization, the very first stargazers sat atop zigzag-shaped towers, called ziggurats, and invented a system to make sense of the stars.

In the beginning, astronomy (the simple study of the stars) and astrology (the study of the stars' influence on people) were the same thing. That's

because the Babylonians—along with the Indians, Chinese, and Native Americans—believed in something called Cosmic Sympathy. They thought that the universe, or cosmos, was so perfectly arranged that every single part was connected to every other part. The Greeks described this link between heaven and Earth best when they said:
"As Above, So Below."

This philosophy led stargazers to look for connections within the heavenly hodgepodge of the sky.

The ancients played connect-the-dots with the stars and "drew" favorite animals and legendary heroes onto the sky. And so the constellations were born. As people continued to watch the sky and record what they saw, they noticed that each spring the constellations were in the same positions they'd been in the previous spring. The same was true for summer, fall, and winter—the movement of the constellations was completely in tune with the seasons. In this way, the stars provided the first calendar, useful for recording important events, planting crops, and keeping holidays. And because of their belief in Cosmic Sympathy, these early people thought that the constellations themselves were powerful—that the stars brought the seasons with them as they shifted across the heavens. The most important of these constellations were the twelve that make up the zodiac: the narrow belt of stars through which the sun, moon, and planets seem to move.

The word "zodiac" comes from the ancient Greek word for "circle of animals."

The first stargazers believed that the sun, moon, and planets were powerful, too, and so they named these heavenly bodies after their mighty gods. Kings and queens appointed astrologers to observe planetary movements and translate their messages. These sky watchers looked for special astral events like eclipses, when the moon seemed to gobble up the sun, or bright spots, when two planets passed just next to each other. They would use these omens, or signs, to tell their leaders whether it was a good day to go into battle, to start work on a new building, or to stay home and nap. Over the years astrologers began using the movements in the sky to learn more about regular people—not just royalty. They found that people born at the same time of year—when the sun is in the same position in the sky—have a lot in common. This gave rise to sun-sign astrology—the same kind of astrology you often see today in newspapers and magazines.

The word "planet" comes from the ancient Greek word for "wanderer."

Of course, nowadays astronomy is a science entirely separate from astrology. But astrologers continue to be fascinated by the possible connections between what happens in

the sky and what happens in our lives here on Earth.

This brings us round to you, dear reader. When you were born, the sun was in the sign of Gemini. The sun, being by far the brightest, hottest, most amazing thing in the sky, stands for your natural gifts—the things you can do while walking backward and chewing gum. It also shows your will— the way you work for what you want.

The fascinating world of astrology can help you make the most of your gifts and talents, strengthen your weak spots, and lead you to a whole lot of fun. But as you ramble through the zodiac zone, remember: The stars are what you make of them. There are as many different types of Geminis as there are Geminis, and you'll always be one of a kind!

HERE'S YOUR MAP

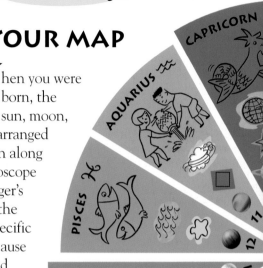

When you were born, the sun, moon, and planets were arranged in a special pattern along the zodiac. A horoscope (one of an astrologer's tools) is a map of the sky pattern at a specific point in time. Because the sun, moon, and planets are always moving at their own speeds, and because the Earth is always spinning, the horoscope changes all the time. (The word "horoscope" comes from the Greek words for "watcher" of the "hour.")

We couldn't include your personal horoscope (because everyone's is different), but you can see

14

where your sun sign falls along the great wheel of the zodiac. Each section shows a sun sign and its name, glyph (a special squiggly mark that stands for the sign), symbol, element, quality, ruling planet, and order in the zodiac—all stuff you'll find out about in this book.

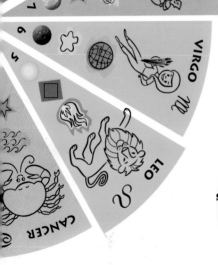

To figure out people's sun signs, look up their birth dates below:
Aries: Mar. 21–Apr. 20
Taurus: Apr. 21–May 20
Gemini: May 21–June 20
Cancer: June 21–July 22
Leo: July 23–Aug. 23
Virgo: Aug. 24–Sept. 22
Libra: Sept. 23–Oct. 23
Scorpio: Oct. 24–Nov. 23
Sagittarius: Nov. 24–Dec. 22
Capricorn: Dec. 23–Jan 21
Aquarius: Jan. 22–Feb. 19
Pisces: Feb. 20–Mar. 20

THE MOON AND PLANETS

Like the sun, the rest of the solar system also influences parts of your character. Think of these heavenly bodies as one big, happy family that's always near to back you up.

FEELINGS: Matched by most ancient cultures with family and the night, caring Mother **MOON** watches over your moods and emotions.

COMMUNICATION: Named after the fast-talking Roman messenger god, Brother **MERCURY** encourages you to express yourself.

BEAUTY: Named for the Roman goddess of love and pleasure, charming Sister **VENUS** shares her great taste in clothes, food, and art.

POWER: Named after the Roman god of war, Brother **MARS** teaches you to stand up for yourself. He inspires you with ambition and energy.

ATTITUDE: Named after the Roman leader of the gods, jovial Uncle **JUPITER** looks at the bright side of life. He reminds you to keep your chin up.

WORK: Named after the Roman god of time, Father **SATURN** is always telling you: "Try harder." His lesson? Doing your best takes time and effort.

IDEAS: Named after the Greek god of the sky, Uncle **URANUS** loves your wild brainstorms. Just look up, and he reminds you: "The sky's the limit!"

DREAMS: Named after the Roman god of the seas, Aunt **NEPTUNE** splashes her magic around. She encourages you to dive into your imagination.

UNDERSTANDING: Named after the Greek god of the underworld, Great-Uncle **PLUTO** is deep. His sensitive smarts help you figure things out.

IT'S ELEMENTARY

Long ago, people thought the world was made of just four elements: fire, earth, air, and water. Though we now know our planet has more than a hundred elements, these first four elements are still astrology's building blocks. In the zodiac, elements stand for personality types.

 FIRE SIGNS are energetic, eager, and proud. Aries, Leos, and Sadges head straight for the action—spreading warmth along the way.

 EARTH SIGNS are no-nonsense, trust-worthy, and successful. Tauruses, Virgos, and Caps make dreams come down-to-earth true.

 AIR SIGNS are cool, idealistic, and social. Geminis, Libras, and Aquarians follow the breeze to fun and friendship.

 WATER SIGNS are caring, artistic, and slightly psychic. Cancers, Scorpios, and Pisces figure out any situation they dive into.

YOUR STAR QUALITY

That's right, every sign has a quality, too: cardinal, fixed, or mutable. A quality relates to the season in which it appears, and stands for a sign's style. Each sign has its own special element-quality combo.

CARDINAL SIGNS begin the seasons. No wonder Aries, Cancers, Libras, and Caps are bursting with creativity. Sometimes pushy, often independent, always ambitious—cardinal kids get noticed.

FIXED SIGNS are cozied up in the middle of each season. That must be why fixed kids are steady, stubborn achievers. Tauruses, Leos, Scorps, and Aquarians never give up on projects or pals.

MUTABLE SIGNS show up when seasons change. Count on Geminis, Virgos, Sadges, and Pisces to be resourceful and flexible. Mutable kids might change directions a lot, but their eyes are always on the prize.

GEMINI IN MYTHOLOGY

Castor and Pollux are the most famous Twins. They were hatched from an egg by their mother Leda. Their father was Zeus, the king of the gods. Masterful Castor was mortal; feisty Pollux was immortal. One day, when the brothers were at battle, Castor was killed. In deepest despair, Pollux prayed to die too. Zeus took pity and brought them both to Mount Olympus, the home of the gods. From there they took turns flying to the heavens to shine in the night sky.

This story holds a key to Gemini's double nature. Half of you is always a true child of the gods, while the other half is a regular, fun-loving kid. Also, the coming and going from Mount Olympus to the skies fits with Twin's master messenger fame. You're always arriving with news from the other side!

BEING A GEMINI

What's new? Gemini knows. If you're born under this merry and mutable air sign, you're the zodiac's shortwave radio. As the best broadcaster on the block, you charm your way into friendships, pranks, and adventure.

Gemini is Latin for "twins," and your glyph is the Roman numeral two. But doesn't it look like a set of antennae? They help you pick up all that vital info.

Your ruler is Mercury, planet of fast talk and fleet feet. Mercury keeps you chock-full of insider chat, funny puns, weird accents, and a million factoids.

Your star challenge? Some call you two-faced when you see two sides to every situation. And you're late a lot. But your worst rap is gossip, the flip side to your charming gift of gab.

Astral advice: Stay put, applying your amazing brain to just *two* great project. And try to tune in to sensitive types who get hurt by your jokes and imitations.

21

GENUINELY GEMINI

The zodiac is rich with thousands of years of history, myths, and legends. Each sign has a treasure of special colors, gems, foods, and more. Here's what's special to (or ruled by) Gemini.

MOTTOS: Don't Fence Me In; I Communicate

RULING PLANET: Mercury

COLORS: Orange, blue

METAL: Quicksilver

BODY AREAS: Arms, hands

GEMS: Aquamarine, crystal, opal

Gemini

STONES: Agate, all striped stones

FLOWERS AND PLANTS: Lavender, woodbine, yarrow

NUMBER: 5

DAY: Wednesday

FOODS: Licorice, all nuts

HERB: Madder

ANIMAL: Monkey, parrot

CITIES: Cardiff, Cordoba, London, Melbourne, San Francisco, Versailles

COUNTRIES: Belgium, Egypt, United States, Wales, all countries on the northeast coast of Africa

NATURE SPOT: Babbling brook

GEMINI ALSO RULES: Messages, news, short trips, talking, Air mail, ambidexterity, bicycling, billboards, cab drivers, computers, school, handwriting, neighbors, pairs, magazines, rumors, traffic

Measuring Up Rulers: In astrology, every sun sign has one ruling planet that keeps an eye out for the sign and protects it. In turn, each sun sign rules many people, places, and things.

23

YOUR KIND OF GEMINI

Like any circle, the zodiac has 360 degrees—giving each of the twelve signs 30 of those degrees. Each sign is further divided into three 10-degree subsigns. These are a combination of the sign with another sign in its element. Which means there are actually three different kinds of Gemini.

All three subsigns remain lively Twins, the Quicksilver Kids of the zodiac, but each one has a slightly different style and goal. Just as Gemini has a ruler—Mercury—Gemini subrulers come from the air signs of Gemini, Libra, and Aquarius. Knowing your subsign helps you make the most of your special talents.

GEMINI-GEMINI

GEMINI-LIBRA

GEMINI-AQUARIUS

FIRST SUBSIGN: GEMINI-GEMINI
MAY 21–MAY 30
RULERS: MERCURY-MERCURY
QUALITIES: MUTABLE-MUTABLE
THE QUICKSILVER MESSENGER

The double Gemini has the fastest feet in the zodiac—just ask the parents and friends who try to keep up with you! A double dose of ramblin' Mercury, planet of high-speed smarts, also gives you one supersonic mind. You pick up information like lint. Being extra mutable, you're extra flexible; if the doldrums hit, you pull some fun from your bag of tricks. Your puns and jokes are wonderfully witty (you love double meanings). Gemini rules the hands—you might use yours when you talk. Or do you save them for playing the guitar?

SECOND SUBSIGN: GEMINI-LIBRA
June 1–June 10
Rulers: Mercury-Venus
Qualities: Mutable-Cardinal
The Spin Doctor

Just as much of a Quicksilver Kid as your neighbor in the first subsign, your liveliness is mellowed by Venus's charm and good taste. This lovey-dovey planet gives you a knack for putting just the right spin on everything you say. Go ahead and brag! The cardinal quality pushes you to make high-flying dreams come true. Finally, Libra gives a fab flair for part-nership and an arty side (you're better at talking about art than most grown-ups). And you do your fair share of dabbling, daubing, and rhyming.

THIRD SUBSIGN: GEMINI-AQUARIUS
June 11–June 20
Rulers: Mercury-Uranus
Qualities: Mutable-Fixed
The Super Kid

You're a shortwave radio, all right. But because Aquarius is such a way-out sign, you tune into news of the weird. Uranus gives flashes of genius (usually around bedtime). The Water Bearer rules friendship, so you're a magnet for ideas that bring the world closer together. The fixed quality makes you the most determined Twin in town. Once you spot a rainbow, you follow it all the way to your pot of gold. And you can always count on Gemini-Aquarius to leap huge problems in a single bound! P.S. Uranus also rules astrology—this book's a cinch for you!

FAMILY MATTERS

Gemini brings snap, crackle, and pop to any family—just ask yours. Life here, like everywhere else, perks up with Twin's mischief and merriment. You like a free-wheeling argument—er, discussion—at dinner, and you make sure all players get in their two cents. (Siblings especially, since your sign is the guardian of brothers and sisters.) Oh, you hate the drudgery of daily chores, but once you get going, tasks bubble along beautifully.

Check out the sibling and parent starguides to maximize your star power on the home front.

Home Sweet Home

SIBLING STARGUIDE

Powerful as the planets are, birth order is important too. Where do you fall in the family lineup?

OLDEST KID: The tots can't begin to keep up—no wonder you get impatient. Good thing your sign bestows a gift for getting along with siblings—once they find you!

YOUNGEST KID: You don't mind being youngest—as long as the old folks have something to teach you. And you magically slip away when they get bossy!

MIDDLE KID: The middle is fine for the zodiac's monkey. You swing up to the older kids, asking questions and listening in. Then you swoop down to the kiddos, sharing discoveries, jokes, and stories.

ONLY KID: You're no fan of long, lonely stretches. As a social butterfly, you need to take your talk talents on tour! Gemini rules neighbors, you know, and you figure out the 'hood fast.

29

PARENT STARGUIDE

Parents are great, yes, but they are adults. For some stellar help with keeping them happy (and getting what you want), look up your parents' sun signs below.

THE ARIES PARENT

This parent is bursting with fiery ideas for fun. Thrilling? Always. Tiring? Not for you. When you want something special, appeal to Aries' weak spot—tell Mom or Pop you'll be first on the block to try it.

THE TAURUS PARENT

Your shenanigans shock the stable Bull, and Taurus's stubbornness beats your endless inventiveness. For far-out favors, make like a fixed sign and act determined. Ask twice, even three times—Bull likes consistency.

THE GEMINI PARENT
This parent shares your bubbling curiosity and is at least as interested in your schoolwork as you. For major missions, crack jokes while explaining your strategy. The Twin likes a cool line of logic and a good laugh.

THE CANCER PARENT
A worrier? Maybe, but Cancer loves fretting over home base. A witty imp like you can only please. For that rock-climbing trip, discuss safety measures and your grown-up guide. And always mention the word "home"—it's music to Crab's ears.

THE LEO PARENT
The generous fire sign treasures your trademark cool and provides a deluxe home base. But cross the majestic king or queen and you'll get a dramatic roar! For the royal seal of approval, appeal to Leo's pride in you—it's huge. (And flattery works like catnip!)

31

THE VIRGO PARENT

Does this down-to-earth sign seem to criticize? Keen-eyed Virgo just sees your potential, and wouldn't want you to waste it. Need permission? Let this picky mom or pop know how carefully you've thought it through. Details are everything to Virgos.

THE LIBRA PARENT

This fellow air sign adores your witty ways and discusses everything with you. One warning: Libra offers a million "what-if's" to every plan. Consider it good training—being single-minded helps you reach the stars.

THE SCORPIO PARENT

This sea-deep water sign fathoms your million and one changes. Just don't try to hide motives—sleuthing Scorp easily sniffs them out. For a gotta-have-it, play up the mystery. Make like a detective on a mission.

THE SAGITTARIUS PARENT

Yowsa! Freedom-loving Sadge guffaws at your winning wit and applauds your talent for juggling a million and one projects. This adds up to starloads of faith in you. For a new adventure, appeal to Archer's sky-high optimism.

THE CAPRICORN PARENT

When your mischief leads to mayhem, Cap "suggests" you point your antennae in a different direction. The Sea-Goat respects hard work and determination. Need a favor? Use the "I've thought long and hard about it" approach.

THE AQUARIUS PARENT

This fellow air sign inspires you with quirky notions and brilliant flashes. You love sharing this parent's high-flying ideals with your pals in the 'hood. In a jam? Tell Aquarius you were only trying to change the world for the better.

THE PISCES PARENT

Congrats, you've won the most indulgent parent in zodiac-ville. But sea-deep Fish can be shocked by your free-and-breezy ways. For a big yes, pour on the syrup—Pisces loves a little sappiness.

CELESTIAL SCHOOL TIPS

Gemini rules school—only one of the reasons you're such a lively student. Teachers respect you because you live for information. Only problem? When you get restless, you pass notes instead of subjects. Use these zodiac pointers to tune back into school.

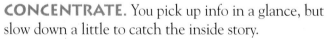

TAKE NOTES. Gemini makes you an ace scribbler. Writing keeps you alert and involved.

GET ORGANIZED. Twin's desk can look like a tornado hit it. Clear the way for new ideas.

CONCENTRATE. You pick up info in a glance, but slow down a little to catch the inside story.

BE ON TIME. Terminally late Gemini drives teacher nuts. And besides, 99 percent of life is just showing up.

TEAM UP. Neighborly Twin works well in groups.

ASTRO ANGLES FOR SPECIFIC SUBJECTS

SCIENCE: Gemini rules technology and computers. Need we say more?

HISTORY: The storyteller in you loves the wild sagas of heroes and battles. And you're great at remembering dates.

SOCIAL STUDIES: Here's the perfect place to practice your awesome debate skills.

MATH: Only problem? You work so quickly that you make simple mistakes. Slow down.

ENGLISH: Creative writing gives you a chance to put some of your tall tales on paper.

LANGUAGES: Twin rules here. Picking up accents is easy for Gemini, and learning a whole language isn't much harder.

Special Gemini Study Tip: You are the one and only sun sign who can do homework while watching TV, talking on the phone, and clipping your toenails. But good luck convincing your parents!

35

ASTRO ACTIVITIES

The original GameBoy—or GameGirl—was born to play. You can easily juggle several sports and hobbies at once. Geminis have a knack for crossing a room or sussing out a game, in a blink of an eye. Some astrologers call you the Artful Dodger. Drives teacher and parents crazy, but it's great for hobbies! Some Geminis skip sports completely and head for the games and puzzles department. When Geminis do take a breather they opt for some reading—any reading. Twin's not picky when it comes to absorbing information (although magazines are your faves).

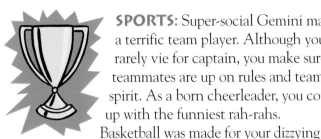

SPORTS: Super-social Gemini makes a terrific team player. Although you rarely vie for captain, you make sure teammates are up on rules and team spirit. As a born cheerleader, you come up with the funniest rah-rahs.

Basketball was made for your dizzying pace. Being in two places at once really throws the opposition, too. The hectic soccer field is a real kick for Twin. In football you prefer running to blocking and tackling. Baseball and softball can get slow unless you're playing first base or shortstop.

For one-on-one and solo sports, try fast-paced racquet games like tennis and ping-pong. Mercury lends you his winged shoes for sprints and hurdles. And your rubber-band flexibility makes you an ace gymnast.

More than just exercise, bike rides around the neighborhood are great info-gathering missions: You always bring home the news! Skates, Rollerblades, and skateboards capitalize on your balance and coordination—and make you feel like you're flying through your element!

HOBBIES: Games like Scrabble and Wheel of Fortune are a natural for the wordsmith in you. Brain

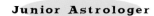

twisters and trivia games give you the mental push-ups you crave. Speedy card games like Spit are Twin-friendly, too.

ART: Pulled any rabbits out of hats lately? The zodiac's trickster is great at magic. And what about comedy routines? Improv is your specialty, since you run your life the way comedians run their shows—making it up as you go along.

And keep those hands in mind: Geminis are great sculptors, musicians, and finger-painters. And don't forget creative writing. (Few Geminis spend time writing about themselves. They invent tales about animals, kids, or other universes.)

HIGH-TECH DELIGHTS: Twin has been known to plop in front of the TV for hours. Once you get that channel changer, you may never leave. And video games are a cinch—you don't like being kicked around on a football field, but you sure clean up on the computerized version. Friendly Gemini rules computers, and you navigate the Internet for data—and chums—from all over the world.

STAR STYLE

CLOTHES: They had better be built for speed. This doesn't mean you live in sweats—trendy Gemini is up on the latest looks.

BEDROOM: You're not messy, exactly. To outside observers your room looks like a gust of fresh air just swept through your books, papers, and games. They're right—that gust is you!

FOOD: Twin's famous for wild food combos. So what if your friends run screaming from your peanut butter-and-sardine sandwiches? Leaves more for you!

MUSIC: It calms you to have tunes going all the time. And what a whiz at lyrics! As pals strain to catch the chorus, you've memorized every tra-la-la and rap.

MOVIES: Anything except ooey-gooey love stories. Comedies are best. Your dead-on impersonations of actors keep pals laughing the next day.

STAR PETS

Some say people choose pets who remind them of themselves—or of the selves they'd like to be. Is it any surprise that Gemini likes birds? Every Twin has a bit of hummingbird flitting about inside. But of all the feathered friends, you prefer the parrot. It talks!

Besides feathered friends, insects come under the rulership of Gemini. They excite your scientific curiosity—you follow those ant farms. Monkeys are also protected by the sign of the Twins, and many Geminis dream of their very own chimp—they'd teach it to roller-skate, carry the phone, and laugh at their jokes.

With normal pets, you want mobility. An Irish setter is light and fast enough to keep up with you, but you'd just love a little Yorkshire terrier to hop into your backpack as you go!

ONE WARNING: Geminis are so busy that they often forget about pets. Don't neglect your furry and feathered friends!

40

FRIENDSHIP ALONG THE ZODIAC TRAIL

Gemini carries the golden key to lifelong popularity: You ask people about themselves, which makes friends feel understood and important. And you're no snob: You'll share a joke with anyone. Yes, Twin has a delightfully light touch, and doesn't sweat the small stuff.

What makes Gemini see double? Crybabies. Spreading your humor usually calms the sentimental sort. But if the tears are terminal, you skip along to the next scene.

Warning: Pals love your spiced-up stories—unless they're about them. Gemini wouldn't blab a secret, but gossip is tempting. Don't! It almost always hurts people.

On your astro-tour of friendships you'll see that every star combo has its ups and downs. You've got so much to teach and learn from each sign, that any duo can work!

> **For a smoother ride on the Zodiac Trail, brush up on your planets (page 16), elements (page 18, and qualities (page 19).**

41

ARIES FRIENDS

DATES: MARCH 21–APRIL 20
SIGN OF THE RAM
RULER: MARS
ELEMENT: FIRE
QUALITY: CARDINAL
SYMBOL: THE RAM'S HORNS

First in the zodiac, Aries tries to come first everywhere else too. Cardinal-fire kids like nothing better than brand-new adventures. Ruled by the warrior Mars, they battle for beliefs. These pals are Red-Hot Chili Peppers! Fortunately, Rams cool down as quickly as they flare up.

You two top the zodiac for ants in the pants. You fuel Ram's energy with wild and woolly schemes, while Aries injects your breezy talk with action. There's no beating around the bush with this *ram*bunctious pal.

Star Wars? You're both famous for dropping projects when bored. Unless you're careful, nothing gets accomplished. And Aries fights mightily when you lock horns. But no matter how hard-headed Ram gets, you two can always have fun together.

TAURUS FRIENDS

DATES: APRIL 21–MAY 20
SIGN OF THE BULL
RULER: VENUS
ELEMENT: EARTH
QUALITY: FIXED
SYMBOL: THE BULL'S HEAD

The first down-to-earth sign in the zodiac, Taurus has a green thumb that works magic on plants, projects, and friends. These fixed-quality beasts rarely brag, and never start stuff without a clear plan. Ruler Venus lends a love of luxury, a fondness for good food, and a laid-back streak. Just call these cuddly kids Teddy Bulls.

Once you've teamed up, the careful, thoughtful Taurus can inspire you to forge ahead when you get bored. Meanwhile, your up-to-the-minute news perks Bull up, especially when it can be put to practical use.

Star Wars? You might complain that this steady friend is too slow. And your butterfly spirit can make Bull see red. But this play-it-safe kid has loads of patience, and stays loyal at the end of the day. As the zodiac's quickest study, stick close to Taurus.

GEMINI FRIENDS

DATES: MAY 21–JUNE 20
SIGN OF THE TWINS
RULER: MERCURY
ELEMENT: AIR
QUALITY: MUTABLE
SYMBOL: THE ROMAN
  NUMERAL TWO

Tuning in to friendship is a breeze these air-sign pals. Ruler Mercury turns up the volume on escapades and laughter. The mutable quality makes these sidekicks born jugglers—Twins work best on two projects at once. And Quicksilver Kids sure can talk a blue streak. (Sound familiar?)

Oh, why do you like this fast-moving, smooth-talking pal so much? Could it be that Gemini is one of the few friends who can keep up with you? Or who has enough outrageous info and hilarious jokes to keep you around? This is one friend you like pairing up with.

Star Wars? Quicksilver Twin changes plans in a flash. And that mimicry—it's entertaining, till Gemini imitates you. But take this friendship at face value and you'll quadruple your fun.

CANCER FRIENDS

DATES: JUNE 21–JULY 22
SIGN OF THE CRAB
RULER: THE MOON
ELEMENT: WATER
QUALITY: CARDINAL
SYMBOL: THE CRAB'S CLAWS

Cancer's moods might change with the moon, but these lunar (not loony!) types always make sure everyone is safe and fed. Count on an elephant's memory—straight A's in history—and worrywart ways. Even if the Moonshine Kid seems shy or dreamy, this cardinal sign has goals galore.

Kindly Crab is a sensitive friend. You say, "I'm Quicksilver cool, I don't need help!" But you can count on Crab to stick by you. In exchange, you involve this caretaker in the latest hubbub. And just watch Crab sinks those claws in!

Star Wars? Cancer's watery worries rain on your parade. (Why must Crab play the zodiac's safety monitor?) Too, Crab gets a little—yes—crabby. In short, Cancer might bug you like your family does. But like family, Crab is always there for you.

LEO FRIENDS

DATES: JULY 23–AUGUST 23
SIGN OF THE LION
RULER: THE SUN
ELEMENT: FIRE
QUALITY: FIXED
SYMBOL: THE LION'S
   MANE AND TAIL

Leo is just your average king of the jungle—dramatic, creative, and loyal. Sun-ruled Lions take center stage, toss their manes about, and then brag about their big deals. But these fixed-quality kids aren't totally self-centered. Leo rules the heart, after all, and theirs are made of pure gold.

Twin and Leo make an extra-friendly duo. This flashy fire sign thrills you—and steadies your spurts of energy. In exchange, you whisk the Lion to new jungles. Together you charm your way into happy hijinks.

Star Wars? No matter how long you've worked together on a project, prideful Leo tends to take the glory. And beware stepping on the Sunshine Kid's super-sensitive feelings with your glib wit. This loyal pal needs you to be true-blue too!

VIRGO FRIENDS

DATES: AUGUST 24–SEPTEMBER 22
SIGN OF THE MAIDEN
RULER: MERCURY
ELEMENT: EARTH
QUALITY: MUTABLE
SYMBOL: "M" WITH ITS TAIL
   CURVING BENEATH IT

Virgos are the zodiac's Nature Kids. Born at harvest time, these earth signs know that it takes patience and hard work to help friendships ripen to perfection. No wonder they're mutable marvels!

Both you Mercury-ruled smarties are loaded with facts and info—but there the similarity ends. Virgo's built with a broad streak of normal, while you worship the new and different. Fortunately, you're a breath of fresh air for this modest mate. Teach your caring friend how humor brightens the world.

Star Wars? While this perfectionist plots and plans, you run screaming, "Dullsville!" But if the criticism bugs you, remember, Virgo just wants everyone to be perfect.

47

LIBRA FRIENDS

DATES: SEPTEMBER 23–OCTOBER 23
SIGN OF THE BALANCE
RULER: VENUS
ELEMENT: AIR
QUALITY: CARDINAL
SYMBOL: THE SCALES

Libra's symbol are the scales of justice, truth, and harmony. Something unfair? These kids cry "foul!" Ruled by Venus, Libras need beauty—ugly places drive them nuts. But don't call them wimps! As cardinal kids, Libras keep iron fists tucked inside their velvet gloves.

You and this fellow chatty air sign hang glide happily. Libra is bewitched by your speed and pizzazz. You're awed by the Talk Show Host's classy tact. And Libra's knack for pairing off makes you a dynamic duo.

Star Wars? Every little breeze tips Libra's balance. When you're dashing on to the next plan, Libra's still dawdling over a million options. But between Twin's juggling and Libra's balancing act, this friendship's bound to be as fun as a three-ring circus!

SCORPIO FRIENDS

DATES: OCTOBER 24–NOVEMBER 23
SIGN OF THE SCORPION
RULER: PLUTO
ELEMENT: WATER
QUALITY: FIXED
SYMBOL: "M" WITH
    SCORPION'S TAIL

Ruled by Pluto, planet of the underworld, Scorpios are magicians: They turn the hairiest mishaps into lucky events. These water signs focus their psychic radar on you with fixed-quality determination. When these Sherlocks give you the thumbs-up, expect lifelong loyalty.

When the zodiac's cub reporter meets this super spy, count on a good story. Your open nature helps Scorp feel secure. And this Pluto pal teaches you a thing or two about keeping mum and finishing fabulous projects.

Star Wars? All those secrets make Twin nervous. But whatever you do, don't blab on Scorp. The only thing that outlasts a Scorpio grudge is a Scorpio friendship!

SAGITTARIUS FRIENDS

DATES: NOVEMBER 24–DECEMBER 22
SIGN OF THE ARCHER
RULER: JUPITER
ELEMENT: FIRE
QUALITY: MUTABLE
SYMBOL: THE ARROW

Ruled by Jupiter, this flaming fire sign's motto is "More, More, More!" Mutable Archers shoot their arrows at all sorts of goals. And thanks to their flexibility and optimism, the Shooting Stars often get bull's-eyes. Don't mistake these jokesters for clowns—Sadges are quick learners and natural teachers.

Gemini and Sadge are horoscope opposites, and you know what they say about opposites. You high-spirited Two Musketeers can get the giggles anywhere. And this buddy won't have any trouble keeping up with your trend-setting ideas or your fast-moving self.

Star Wars? Even Gemini has one up on Archer in the tact department. Poor Sadge doesn't know how much those arrows of truth can sting. But you can always depend on this straight-shooting pal for fun.

CAPRICORN FRIENDS

DATES: DECEMBER 23–JANUARY 21
SIGN OF THE SEA-GOAT
RULER: SATURN
ELEMENT: EARTH
QUALITY: CARDINAL
SYMBOL: HORNS OF THE
   GOAT, TAIL OF THE FISH

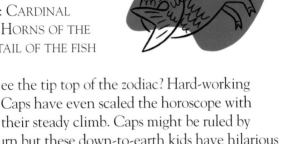

See the tip top of the zodiac? Hard-working Caps have even scaled the horoscope with their steady climb. Caps might be ruled by stern Saturn but these down-to-earth kids have hilarious senses of humor. Don't expect to see Caps trotting off in wacky directions. They like their view from the top.

Gemini is a little puzzled by the mighty Captain Zodiac. This earth sign takes everything so seriously. But you love puzzles! Besides, you can absorb some of this pal's steadiness. Meanwhile, share your happy-go-lucky world view with this earthy friend.

Star Wars? Capricorn plays Billy Goat Gruff to your Peter Pan and may tell you to grow up. Smart Gemini just giggles when Cap pulls the snob routine. Pretty soon Cap's guffawing, too.

AQUARIUS FRIENDS

DATES: JANUARY 22–FEBRUARY 19
SIGN OF THE WATER BEARER
RULER: URANUS
ELEMENT: AIR
QUALITY: FIXED
SYMBOL: WAVES OF WATER

Expect the unexpected. Aquarians are stubborn freethinkers, armed with unusual remedies for the world's problems. These fixed-air kids are powered by Uranus, planet of sudden change; they pour their shocking ideas over everyone. (Aquarius is the sign of friendliness.)

Look alive, Gemini! Hanging with the Shock Jock keeps you on your toes. You like this pal's independence and shake-'em-up ideas. Aquarius loves your quirky ways and treats your dilemmas with smart logic. Best of all, you can count on starloads of new pals spinning into Water Bearer's orbit.

Drawbacks? Fixed-quality Aquarius seeks the single, one-and-only truth, while mutable you see at least two truths. But when the two of you air-heads hook up, you're in for a whirlwind of excitement.

PISCES FRIENDS

DATES: FEBRUARY 20–MARCH 20
SIGN OF THE FISH
RULER: NEPTUNE
ELEMENT: WATER
QUALITY: MUTABLE
SYMBOL: TWO FISH

Pisces are the zodiac's dreamers. Like their symbol of two fish swimming in opposite directions, these sensitive water signs are slightly divided. Being mutable, they keep their options open! Ruler Neptune adds a glamorous glow and wild imagination—Fish makes life one huge art project.

You two are super flexible. No one can pin Pisces or you down to any one position. You're inspired by the Dreamboat Kid's endless creativity, and downright delighted by the famous faith in friendship. Meanwhile, Fish is dazzled by your high spirits and cleverness.

Star Wars? Sensitive Pisces lets one hitch snag the whole month. This is nuts to a juggler like you. When one ball drops, you've got five others to play with. The Fish's deep-sea feelings might make you want to scram. But tune into Pisces wavelength for an oceanful of fun.

SIGNS OF LOVE

Congratulations, Twin! You're the zodiac's best flirt. You fall in love (or will someday) in the same way you do everything else—with a light, charming touch. You don't bother with gushy love notes. Your beloveds are your buddies first.

As the Artful Dodger you're awfully good at playing hard to get. (Once in a while you have a crush on two people at once!) But your true sweetheart must have the smarts to keep your quicksilver mind hopping.

Here's a glimpse at how your romances might shape up along the zodiac trail.

ARIES: Great balls of fire! This charmer almost leaves you speechless. You two appreciate each other's humor. Flare-ups die down quickly, with no sore feelings; you just race on to more adventure. The Perfect Plan: A sports event.

TAURUS: The Bull is wowed by your cool smarts and, in return, offers steady support when you're frazzled. Any problems? If it gets too steady, Twin gets bored. The Perfect Plan: A walk outdoors while sharing snacks.

GEMINI: Talk about doubling your pleasure! Smitten by flirtatious Twin, you giggle your way to good times. A fab pairing, if the jester isn't juggling several admirers. The Perfect Plan: A trip to an amusement park, or hanging at the corner magazine rack.

CANCER: Most days you cherish the kindest homebody in the zodiac. But a Crab with hurt feelings will scuttle away— for good. The Perfect Plan: Hanging out at home, especially if cooking's involved.

LEO: Your instant attraction to the swaggering Lion can last beyond that first spark. Just don't mess with the pride of the Leo, or you'll be the one burning. The Perfect Plan: A party where Leo can make a grand entrance.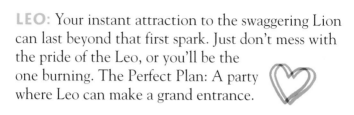

VIRGO: Kind Virgo is awed by your cheery charm, and nurses your wounds should you fall from the heights. But all that thinking can make you reach for your bungee cords. The Perfect Plan: A megabookstore where you can explore, read, and snack.

LIBRA: Here's a sweetie who can keep up with your nimble noggin. Venus-ruled Libra injects romance—showing you what relationships are all about. The Talk Show Host is clingier than Gemini, but you two find the balance. The Perfect Plan: Painting, dancing, or shopping for clothes.

SCORPIO: Sure, the secretiveness bugs you—and forget the jealousy. But Scorp runs the zodiac's department of mysterious attraction, so you might be hooked. The Perfect Plan: An afternoon of brainteasers and games.

SAGITTARIUS: Archer likes anything that involves exploring new horizons and a lot of laughs. (Sound familiar?) Count on a far-out destination—and when you two take the high road, boredom can't survive. The Perfect Plan: A rollicking bus trip downtown.

CAPRICORN: Going steady is exactly what Twin and this clever earth sign do—climbing the mountain of romance at an even pace. Just make sure you don't end up with blisters! The Perfect Plan: Hiking, or just strolling a bookstore's aisles.

AQUARIUS: Go on and let Water Bearer rock your world. This pairing makes for fast times and exciting days, unless this freethinker confuses you with just any old friend. The Perfect Plan: A trip to a busy game arcade at the mall.

PISCES: This charmer is a bit bashful, but the glamorous glow keeps your interest strong. You treasure time spent figuring out the Pisces puzzle. The Perfect Plan: Feeding the ducks or making arts and crafts at home.

GEMINI ALL GROWN UP

You'll have two cars, two degrees, and two pets, along with five or six titles on your business cards. You'll change your mind about your career again and again. But in the end, you're sure to come up with a life plan that combines your lightning-fast smarts and your juggling skills. You relax when both phone lines are blinking, a fax is coming in, two people are knocking on your door, and you have a list of ten things to do before the day is out. You'll probably be able to gab yourself into any job you interview for. So make sure you want it!

Here's a list of things a happy Gemini's career—or careers—must include:

COMMUNICATION: It's your chief talent, and it is powerful. Your highest goal is to communicate messages that inspire people.

TEACHING AND LEARNING: Remember that radio transmitter. You'll be absorbing as well as sharing what comes your way.

HUSTLE AND BUSTLE: Even if you live way out in the country, you'll whip up a flurry of action wherever you go.

VARIETY: If your job doesn't have it, you create it. That could mean promotion or a big mess!

TRAVELING: With rambling Mercury as your ruler, fun road trips play a big part in your life.

TRADITIONAL GEMINI FIELDS
- Comedy
- Music
- Politics
- Postal work
- Public relations
- Reporting, broadcasting, editing
- Teaching
- Telecommunications, computer operations
- Transport: driver, pilot
- Traveling sales
- Writing

GEMINI HALL OF FAME

"Do I contradict myself?
Very well then I contradict myself,
(I am large, I contain multitudes.)
—Walt Whitman, poet

Each of these Gemini achievers made the most of his or her star-given talents.

Margaret Bourke-White
    (*photographer, writer*)
George Washington Carver
    (*chemist, inventor, naturalist*)
James Brown (*soul singer*)
Jacques Cousteau (*oceanographer*)
Miles Davis (*jazz trumpeter*)
Johnny Depp (*actor*)
Sir Arthur Conan Doyle (writer)
Isadora Duncan (*dance innovator*)
Bob Dylan (*singer, songwriter, poet*)
Ralph Waldo Emerson (*poet, philosopher*)
M.C. Escher (*graphic artist*)
Melissa Etheridge (*musician*)
Anne Frank (*writer, The Diary of Anne Frank*)

Gemini

Paul Gauguin *(painter)*
Steffi Graf *(tennis champion)*
Marvin Hamlish *(Broadway composer)*
Patrick Henry *(American patriot)*
John F. Kennedy *(U.S. president)*
Paul McCartney *(musician, Beatles member)*
Marilyn Monroe *(actress)*
Bill Moyers *(TV journalist)*
Mike Myers *(comedian, actor)*
Peter the Great *(Russian tzar, crowned Emperor)*
The artist formerly known as Prince *(musician)*
Sally Ride *(U.S. astronaut)*
Jeanette Rankin *(first female U.S. congresswoman)*
Jane Deeter Rippin *(head, American Girl Scouts)*
Maurice Sendak *(children's writer)*
Brooke Shields *(model, actress)*
Beverly Sills *(opera singer)*
Aung San Suu Kyi *(Burmese human rights activist)*
Jim Thorpe *(legendary Native American athlete)*
Frank Lloyd Wright *(visionary architect)*
W.B. Yeats *(poet, mystic)*

GALACTIC GIFT GUIDE

ARIES likes anything new. Hats, model cars, tools, sports gear. Colors: Red, white, and see-through.

The best gifts for **TAURUS** show good taste or taste good: cookies, socks, plants. Colors: All shades of green.

Make it fun—like **GEMINI**. Pick games, joke books, or magic tricks. Colors: Orange—anything bright!

A card with a photo of the two of you, antiques, pillows, or food is perfect for **CANCER**. Colors: Anything silvery or shimmery.

Take **LEO** out! Also: Movie tickets, CDs, hair accessories. Colors: Gold, red, orange, and yellow.

For **VIRGO** keep it simple and neat: all-natural products, how-to books, computer games. Colors: Yellow-green, earthy colors, and white.

The best gift for **LIBRA** is your company. Also: Music, books, flowers, clothes, and sweets. Colors: Mauve and pastels; red for special days.

Slip **SCORPIO** the gift on the sly, or have a treasure hunt for a detective book, a magic or science kit, or art supplies. Colors: Maroon, deep blue, and green.

Bring **SADGE** to a room full of rowdies. Try tickets to a game or special event, maps, and sci-fi stuff. Colors: Purple, royal blue, white, and anything Day-Glo.

Appeal to **CAP'S** big goals: a pen set, biographies of famous folks, helium balloons. Colors: Navy blue, earth tones, and silver.

AQUARIUS likes science experiments, high-tech gear, anything striped—just make sure it's a surprise! Colors: Sky blue, shocking blue or yellow, even neon.

PISCES wants magic. Snatch up a book of poetry, pictures, sunglasses, or candles. Colors: Pale blue-green, white, silver, and purple.

AMAZING THINGS WILL HAPPEN TO YOU!

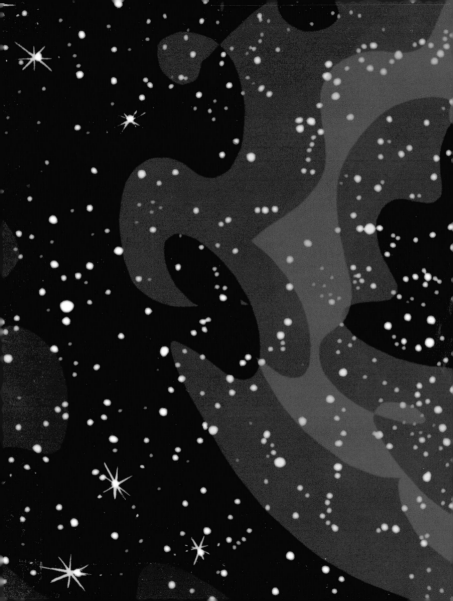